Activities to Help Impulsive Children

by Loretta Oleck Berger, MSW

Childswork
ChildsPLAY
CALL 1·800·962·1141

Calm Down & Play
Activities to Help Impulsive Children

by Loretta Oleck Berger, MSW

Childswork/Childsplay publishes products for mental health professionals, teachers, and parents who wish to help children with their developmental, social, and emotional growth. For questions, comments, or to request a free catalog describing hundreds of games, toys, books, and other counseling tools, call 1-800-962-1141.

© 2003 Childswork/Childsplay, LLC
A Guidance Channel Company
1-800-962-1141
www.GuidanceChannel.com

ISBN 1-58815-055-0

TABLE OF CONTENTS

Introduction

A lot of energy goes into working with any child...and a lot more energy may be demanded if you are working with an impulsive child or a child diagnosed with Attention Deficit Hyperactivity Disorder. Life with such a child is not easy. It is not calm, and it is not quiet. It can be frustrating and challenging. BUT...it can also be spontaneous, animated, lively, exciting, and humorous.

Games and play are the most effective ways to engage a child's interest. If you are a professional therapist counseling impulsive children, you may already use some play techniques with your clients. If you are a parent or an adult working with children in a nontherapeutic role, it is not likely that you have a repertoire of activities specifically geared towards the unique needs of these children. This book was created to give parents and professionals a variety of fun, easy-to-follow, creative, and educational activities to help children ages five to twelve learn to modify their behaviors.

The activities were chosen because they are easy to implement, do not require many materials, and are not costly. Most take no more than ten minutes from start to finish. You can play most of these games anywhere, which means that you have the potential to help a child while waiting on line at the supermarket, sitting at the dinner table, driving in the car, or traveling on the bus—as well as in therapeutic sessions.

Whether you are a mental health professional, a teacher, a parent, or a caregiver, you can use the effective behavioral strategies and simple activities in this book to help children toward better self-control, higher self-esteem, improved organizational skills and longer attention spans—all while having fun! The activities are organized into five chapters targeting different behaviors and specific traits, as follows:

1. For calming down and controlling impulses
2. For learning to focus, concentrate, and organize thoughts
3. For identifying and verbalizing feelings
4. For building self-esteem and confidence
5. For channeling and releasing excess energy appropriately

Select activities according to the child's interests and the specific skills you want to work on. If the child does not want to participate in the chosen activity, move on to a different one. Do not take complete control of these activities and do not expect the child to do what he is not capable of; that will set him up for increased frustration. These activities will only be beneficial if the interaction between adult and child is enjoyable and entertaining, and remember—have patience, perspective, and a sense of humor!

NOTE:
The pronoun "he" has been used because boys are much more likely than girls to have A.D.D. or A.D.H.D. By no means does the use of "he" minimize the fact that girls also have A.D.D and A.D.H.D.

Chapter 1:
For Calming Down and
Controlling Impulses

Impulsive children tend to become overly aroused, and they are easily provoked to excessive motion and emotion. The activities in this chapter can help a child relax his body and calm his energies. If you initiate these exercises on a regular basis, the child will eventually learn to use them independently to prevent build-up of daily stress. A.D.H.D. is often marked by behaviors such as fidgeting, squirming, impulsiveness, and difficulty in judging appropriate physical boundaries. The child may appear to be on the go constantly, wearing out everyone around him. Excessive stimulation and stress may cause him to become overemotional.

What do parents often do with kids in these situations? Too often, they may plop them in front of the TV to try and distract them. This chapter aims to teach the child how to tune in to what his body is doing and feeling, so that he develops a keener consciousness of the tension and relaxation of his muscles. As he becomes more conscious of his movement, balance, and posture, he will better be able to identify specific areas of tension that need to be soothed or calmed. Ultimately, he will feel much more in control of his bodily processes and motor planning. From a social standpoint, these activities will also help to foster the child's awareness of appropriate personal space and boundaries.

#1 The Breathing Balloon

Therapeutic Objective

To provide the child with a sense of internal control, and promote relaxation, self-control, and body awareness

Activity

One thing a child can easily control is his own breathing. Have the child take deep breaths, inhaling through his nose and exhaling through his mouth. To help the child focus, suggest that he close his eyes and take a few moments to concentrate on his breathing, until he can hear it and feel it. Ask him to sense his body expanding with air, as if it were a balloon. The more deep breaths he takes, the bigger the balloon becomes. Ask what color the balloon is. How big is it? As big as a boulder? A house? As wide as the ocean? As tall as a mountain? Ask him to describe what he is imagining. Remind him to breathe and not hold his breath. Suggest that he does not want the balloon to pop, so he should let the air out to deflate the balloon. Slowly and calmly, encourage the child to concentrate on breathing in and out, as his tension releases and his entire body sinks into deep relaxation.

More to Think About

When a child exhibits hyperactive behavior, you can remind him not to pop like a balloon. Encourage him to remember this exercise and use it to regain control over his body. Remind him to breathe slowly, inhaling through his nose and exhaling through his mouth, deflating all the excess air in the balloon, and releasing the excess energy from his body. This activity is particularly good to calm a child at bedtime and ease him into sleep.

#2 Robot/Rag Doll

Therapeutic Objective

To enable the child to master control over his body and actions

Activity

Ask the child to stiffen and tense his body as if he were a robot, and walk around the room using stiff and jerky robot motions. You might suggest that the child speak using a robot voice, and as a robot, engage in a variety of typical activities, such as writing his name or catching a ball. Then, ask the child to act like a rag doll, completely relaxed. Have the child walk around the room, talk, take deep breaths and relax, stand up from a seated position, and skip or jump like a rag doll.

Ask the child to describe what happened to his body when he was acting like a robot. What did it feel like to be a rag doll? Can he find a balance? Explain that balance is a place in the middle—not too floppy and not too stiff. What does the balance feel like? Does it feel natural or forced? Is it easier to stand, sit, stretch, and do daily activities in this balanced place? Can he draw a picture of a rag doll and a robot? Look at the differences in the picture.

More to Think About

If a child will not sit at the dinner table—slipping off the chair, rolling on the floor, getting up too many times—you can remind him of this exercise. You might ask him to eat like a robot with a stiff body. Next, ask him to eat like a rag doll, and then try to find the balance in the middle. When he has found the middle, he will be neither too tense nor too floppy. This activity will help the child identify and become more aware of his own inner balance.

Look for stiff, rigid materials in your environment. Have the child touch them. What do they feel like? Now find loose, floppy materials. Compare and contrast the differences to help the child integrate external sensations with internal feelings.

#3 Sleepy Animals

Therapeutic Objective
To ease the child's transition to sleep

Activity
Ask the child to make believe he is a cat. What does he look like? Is he furry or sleek? A Persian, a tabby, or a Siamese? Have the child lie down on a carpet, bed, or mat, stretching and yawning like a cat. Tell him to get on all fours, push his back up towards the ceiling, and then arch his back. What makes a cat sleepy? How does a cat sleep? In a ball? Stretched out?

What other sleepy animal can he pretend to be? Encourage the child to act like the sleepy animal he has chosen. How does that animal look when he is tired? Where does he sleep?

More to Think About
You may want to put a few pictures or names of animals in a bag. Have the child choose one and pretend to be that animal.

This exercise can help a child who is having trouble winding down for bed. You can ask him to curl up his body like a cat going to sleep. Can he make a quiet, purring sound? Try stroking his head, or scratching or massaging his back. The physical touch may help to relax and center the child.

#4 The Elevator

Therapeutic Objective
To help the child control his feelings

Activity
Begin by asking the child to imagine he is stepping inside a warm, safe elevator that is slowly moving down. The top floor represents wild, impulsive or out-of-control behavior, and the first floor feels the most secure, balanced and calm. Ask him which floor he feels he is starting on. Then ask him to feel the elevator slowly descending. Explain that the more the elevator moves down, the more relaxed his body feels. The child can go up in his elevator and experience a more active, out-of-control feeling, but the challenge is to bring the elevator down to ground level, where there is a sense of calm and comfort.

If you are a parent using this activity with a younger child, have him sit on your lap. Tell him that he is in an elevator. Ask him how many floors the elevator has. Even if the child says two, you can continue the activity. Holding the child and moving your legs with increasing speed, say, "Going up, up, up, and getting wild." Slowing your legs, say, "Going down, down, down, and feeling calmer, feeling relaxed. Take a deep breath." Encourage the child to feel quiet and peaceful. Suggest that he try to hold his body still and relaxed when the elevator arrives at the first floor.

More to Think About
When a child's behavior is restless and impulsive, remind him of the elevator and ask him which floor he is on. What does it feel like? Ask him to slowly come down to a lower floor. Parents may ask a younger child to sit on their lap for an elevator ride. An older child may respond more effectively if you challenge him to come down to the first floor independently.

It may be helpful to draw an elevator on a rectangular piece of paper, giving each floor a different picture or symbol. For example, the tenth floor may be a lightning storm, the ninth floor a thundercloud and so on, until the first floor, which may be a picture of a calm ocean. You can use the picture as a visual reference to help the child identify his feelings. Next to the first floor on the picture, write a special treat, such as getting a sticker, watching a special video, or having a book read to him. When the child is able to come down to the first floor on his own, he can receive that treat.

#5 The Honey Jar

Therapeutic Objective
To teach the child that he can control his body speed and movements

Activity
Ask the child to make believe he is inside a honey jar. Ask him to move in the honey. How does it feel to walk? To push with his arms? To turn around? What does it sound like? What does it taste like?

Honey is sticky, making movement more difficult and much slower. The idea of using arms and legs in honey creates resistance in the body and fosters an awareness of muscle tension and release that will naturally slow down the child's movements. When the child needs to gain more control over his body movements or his restlessness, this exercise will remind him of slow motion behavior.

More to Think About
With the child, brainstorm a list of other substances that may slow him down, such as Jell-O or glue. It is often easier for a child to evoke a feeling when he has used a variety of senses; if you are doing this activity at home, go into the kitchen and have the child touch these sticky, gooey substances. You might also discuss various environments where it is appropriate to slow down physically. You can reinforce self-control by reminding the child to approach others as if he were walking in honey, gently and slowly. It may feel unnatural to move slowly at first, but over time it will become more comfortable.

#6 Visualization of a Special Place

Therapeutic Objective

To provide the child with a safe, comforting internalized environment that will help him calm down

Activity

Ask the child to close his eyes and imagine he is at a special place, such as a beach, a mountain, or a river. The place can be one he has seen, or an imaginary place. Tell the child to take three slow, deep breaths, in through his nose and out through his mouth. Now, quietly ask him some questions about his special place. What does this place look like? What does it smell like? Does it have a name? If not, ask the child to make up a name for it. Speaking slowly and clarifying details, you can then guide the child on a journey through this special place. What does it feel like? Is there anyone with him? Who? What is he doing there? Why is it special? What feelings does he have in this place? Does he feel safe and calm?

Explain to the child that he can go to this place in his imagination whenever he needs to calm down.

More to Think About

The child can draw a picture or cut one out of a magazine to represent his special place. When the child needs to calm down, show him the picture to remind him of his special place and ask if he wants to travel there in his imagination.

#7 Relaxing Retreat

Therapeutic Objective
To enable the child to feel in control of his emotions

Activity
Make a special, safe place where the child can go to calm down. It could be a tree house, a tent, or even the corner of a closet. Allow the child to choose relaxing things to keep in his retreat. You might suggest items, such as a pillow, a book, photos of good friends, the scrapbook described later in activity #35, or a favorite stuffed animal or doll.

When you notice that the child is overstimulated, bored, or aggressive or that his behavior is beginning to escalate, suggest that he go to his relaxing retreat.

More to Think About
Put a shoebox containing small surprises in the child's retreat. You might include some crayons and paper, or some little toy figures to play with. An older child might like baseball cards, a snack, a new music tape, or art supplies. When the child needs to calm down or be redirected, tell him to relax in his retreat and to look inside the shoebox. The novelty of what you have selected will help engage him in a more purposeful activity.

8 The Statue Game

Therapeutic Objective

To help the child remain more focused and aware of appropriate behaviors and boundaries

Activity

Ask the child to be a statue, standing as still as possible and trying not to move at all. Count or use a watch to time how long the child can stand like a statue. You can have a contest with the child to see who can remain still for a longer period of time, or you can have the child try to beat the clock. Set a timer for a reasonable amount of time for the child, ranging from five seconds to a few minutes.

To vary the game, take turns trying to make the "statue" laugh. Whoever can keep from laughing for a longer time wins the game.

More to Think About

A good time to suggest playing this game is when you see the child's energy level rising and sense that he is beginning to feel out of control. Each time you play, the child is improving his ability to remain still and calm for longer periods of time, and becoming better able to understand that he is capable of controlling himself. Keep a chart to record the child's progress.

For an educational twist, ask the child to be a well-known statue or monument, such as the Statue of Liberty or the Eiffel Tower. Explore with the child where the statue or monument is located and why it was erected. What does it represent? Why is it famous?

You can also play this game as sculptor and sculpture. One person is the sculptor and shapes the other person into a statue, who tries to guess what he is a statue of. The roles are then reversed, with the statue becoming the sculptor.

#9 The Turtle

Therapeutic Objective
To provide an alternative to aggressive behavior and teach the concept of personal boundaries

Activity
Ask the child to visualize himself as a turtle with a big shell on his back. Have the child imagine that his movements are slow and quiet, like a turtle's. Suggest that he bring his arms and legs in close to his body, shorten his neck, bring his head downward, and move slowly. Then, ask him to walk around the room like a turtle, or play a game feeling like a turtle. Ask him to try feeling like a turtle for a specific period of time. What does it feel like? Try placing a large bag of rice or beans on the child's back, as if it were a shell. The weight will help the child feel more contained.

Together, think of other slow-moving, gentle, contained animals, and have the child pretend to be those animals.

More to Think About
If the child is having difficulty in his classroom, for example, due to lack of impulse control, this activity can be very helpful. Give the child a reminder of the activity to take to school—perhaps a photo of a turtle or even the word "turtle" written on a piece of paper.

The visualization and physical characteristics of this game can help a younger child learn to contain aggression, rather than act out impulsively. For a child who may act out aggressively with other children, reinforce your expectations that he will be gentle by reminding him to be a turtle, keeping his hands to himself and containing his impulses. With his arms stiff and drawn inward, it is impossible for him to lash out.

#10 What Happens When...?

Therapeutic Objective
To help the child internalize the concept that his actions cause reactions

Activity
Take turns making up a situation where it is important that the child control his behavior, and giving the consequence. For example, you might ask, "What happens when you run in the halls at school?" The child then gives an answer, such as "I might hurt myself or someone else." Then it's the child's turn to ask the question. The situations can be serious or funny. For example, you might ask, "What happens when you are at a fancy restaurant, and you put your pet frog on the table?"

More to Think About
This activity can be played anywhere at any time. If there are specific behaviors you want to target with the child, keep the tone light by mixing them in with others that don't relate to him.

#11 When...Then... Penny Toss

Therapeutic Objective

To strengthen the child's understanding that there are consequences to specific behaviors

Activity

This activity will help the child understand the concept that there is an order to what happens. When he makes a choice or follows a specific direction, then something else—either negative or positive—will naturally occur.

At varying distances on the floor, set up some easy targets, perhaps small pieces of paper or plastic cups. Standing a few feet away, the first person tosses a penny at the targets. When the penny touches or lands in a target, the person states a "When..." situation; then, the second person has to state the consequence. For example, you toss a penny and it lands in a cup. At this point, you might say, "When I am calm..." Then it is the child's turn to toss his penny and add the consequence: "When I am calm, then I can focus on my homework." Now switch places, having the child come up with a "when" situation and the adult say what would happen.

More to Think About

Make a list of "When...then..." situations and post it in a place that the child sees often. The more he reads it and is aware of the consequences of behaviors, the more he can internalize the "When...then..." formula.

At home, you can use this activity when playing basketball. Whoever makes a basket first gets to come up with the situation.

CHAPTER 2:
For Learning to Focus, Concentrate, and Organize Thoughts

Inattention and distractibility are two components that describe an impulsive child. He may have difficulty remaining on task and paying attention. He may be distracted by external stimuli—conversations, toys, computers, or television—or internal stimuli, such as thoughts, daydreams, or feelings. The activities in this chapter serve two purposes:

1. To encourage children to better focus, concentrate and organize their thoughts by sorting, discussing, counting, comparing and contrasting data
2. To help children learn frustration tolerance and the ability to remain attentive and focused on a task, whether it is simple or difficult

Children may find these activities easy or highly challenging. And even if the child finds the specific task simple, he may find remaining attentive to the task extremely challenging. The activities in this chapter are less about perfecting the outcome than about learning to focus on a structured, purposeful task. They emphasize all five senses, because each child has a different learning style that influences his focus, attention, concentration, and organization. A child who has difficulty following verbal cues may easily respond to visual cues. A child who has difficulty remembering the alphabet song may remember his letters after touching the rough feel of letters cut from sandpaper.

When doing these activities at home, minimize external distraction by selecting a quiet environment. Avoid a playroom where the child might be

tempted by his toys. Keep the radio and television off. If external noise becomes so intrusive that the child's functioning is significantly impaired, consider purchasing a white noise machine to muffle sounds. For internal distractions, you can remind the child to get back on track by setting an egg timer or a beeper to sound every five or ten minutes. The more organized, structured, and routinized his environment, the easier time the impulsive child will have at home and at school.

#12 Sort It Out

Therapeutic Objective
To teach the child to organize information logically

Activity
Ask the child to sort and arrange collections of items by size, shape, color, and/or composition. You can use items such as buttons, seashells, jellybeans, or loose change, and an empty egg carton works well as a container. After the child has sorted and arranged the collection, ask him to describe what he's done and what he sees. Depending upon the child's age and abilities, you can count the objects, add and subtract them, label them, and/or compare and contrast them.

More to Think About
This activity can also be done outside, where the child can find sticks, leaves, pebbles, etc. He can use these materials to create a collage, arranging the materials by size, shape, color and/or composition.

Arrange the materials into letter shapes to teach the younger child to recognize the letters of the alphabet. A child who finds it difficult to remain attentive to academic tasks may enjoy learning letters by touching the various textures of the different objects.

#13 Seeing Patterns

Therapeutic Objective
To foster spatial awareness and sharpen thought processes by strengthening the child's ability to decipher patterns

Activity
Use items such as buttons, pebbles, checkers, or candies to make a pattern, e.g., one red checker, two black checkers, one red checker, and so on. Take turns copying or finishing each other's pattern. Depending upon the child's age and ability, you can actually practice the pattern or you can just look at each other's pattern for one minute. Then, cover your patterns and try to re-create each other's pattern from memory. Whoever can do it first wins!

More to Think About
You can work with patterns every day, slowly making them more intricate and difficult. Being aware of patterns opens up a myriad of other activities and possibilities. Ask the child to find patterns outside the window as you are driving somewhere. Look for patterns on the tiles of floors, in wallpaper designs, in fabrics, and in the natural environment.

As suggested in activity #12, a child may organize his thoughts more efficiently if he is able to touch the patterns. After creating patterns with various materials, share in the sensory aspect of touching the pattern, feeling its roughness, smoothness, bumpiness, or sleekness. The tactile element will help reinforce the idea of patterns and organization, and it will also help sharpen the child's observation skills.

#14 Picture Details

Therapeutic Objective
To improve the child's attention and observational skills through the development of visual memory

Activity
Choose a drawing, photograph, or book illustration with a variety of details. Have the child look at the picture for one minute. Then, ask the child to remember as many details as possible from the picture, and draw or list them from memory.

More to Think About
Picture Details can be used anywhere to help children calm down and to encourage them to pay better attention to detail. Parents can use the activity any time—waiting at a restaurant or a doctor's office, or standing on line. If you don't have a picture, you can use anything in the environment, such as a bowl filled with fruit, a table set for dinner, or a landscape. This activity engages a child's visual abilities by encouraging attention to detail.

15 Questions and Answers

Therapeutic Objective
To strengthen listening skills, auditory processing, and auditory memory

Activity
First, make up a simple question. The child has to answer your question and then make up a question of his own. The one rule is that the child must use the last letter of the previous answer as the first letter of his answer. Here's an example:

> Question: What is the opposite of left?
> Answer: Right.

Since "t" is the last letter of the word "right," the answer to the next question must begin with the letter "t." For example:

> Question: What is white and in your mouth?
> Answer: Teeth.

The next question will have an answer that begins with the letter "h."

More to Think About
Geared toward an older child who knows how to spell, this exercise is great to play on a long car ride. As a variation of this game, have a conversation with the child about any topic, with one rule: players must begin each sentence with the next letter of the alphabet, beginning with the letter "A." As an example:

Child: **A**lligators are cool.
Adult: **B**ut they can be dangerous.
Child: **C**an you tell the difference between an alligator and a crocodile?
Adult: **D**efinitely, by the shape of their nose.

The above conversation went from "A" to "D." See how many letters you can get through in alphabetical order.

#16 I Spy—with Five Senses

Therapeutic Objective
To help the child develop a greater sense of detail and become more aware of how his environment affects his emotions and behavior

Activity
This activity is the familiar game of "I Spy"—with an educational and effective new twist. Using all five senses, it encourages the child to label various stimuli in his environment and learn to identify how they directly affect him.

The child or adult says, "I spy something that..." The other player must look around and guess what the speaker has spied. Each player has three guesses to figure it out.

Below are examples of "I Spy," using each of the five senses—smell, sound, taste, touch, and sight:

> I spy something that smells sour. (a lemon)
> I spy something that sounds like "toot-toot." (a toy train)
> I spy something that tastes sweet. (a cookie)
> I spy something that feels fluffy. (a cotton ball)
> I spy something red. (an apple)

More to Think About
This is another activity that can be played anywhere, at any time. Using all five senses stimulates the child's awareness of his environment and his physical processes and sensations.

17 Five Senses Exploration

Therapeutic Objective

To develop the child's understanding of his senses and awareness of his own body in its environment

Activity

Label each of five bags (or other containers) for one of the five senses. In each bag, place a few items that specifically correlate to that sense. Describe the five senses to the child. With eyes closed or wearing a blindfold, the child will use his senses to guess the items.

In the "smell" bag, you might put a flower, cheese, perfume, and a lemon. Ask the child to describe what he smells. Is it sour? Is it sweet? Does he like that aroma? Does it remind him of anything else?

In the "touch" bag, you can put sandpaper, cotton balls, an ice cube in a plastic bag, a sponge, and an emery board. Is the object rough? Bumpy? Soft? Hot? Cold? Suggest that the child rub the item on the back of his hand to feel the texture.

In the "hearing" bag, you can put items that make noise, such as pieces of sandpaper to scratch together, a small musical instrument, a bell, two sticks to tap together, or newspaper to crumple. Is the sound soft? Loud? Pleasing or annoying? Can the child imitate that sound with his voice?

In the "sight" bag, have the child guess what an object looks like by touching it before he takes it out of the bag. Ask the child to describe the object in visual terms. Is it is colorful? Is it round or square? Then have him take the item out of the bag and describe what he sees. Does it look beautiful? Ugly? Dull? Is the object what he imagined?

In the "taste" bag put candy, popcorn, a lemon slice, etc. Does it taste sweet? Sour? Delicious?

More to Think About

Take the child on a "sense" hunt indoors or outdoors. Use the five senses to distinguish various stimuli. Stop and smell the flowers, or touch the earth. Look at some pictures. Listen to a classical music CD. Taste a lemon.

Try using senses in a different way. Have the child touch things with his feet. Try placing an object against his cheek or against his back. Does it feel different in different places?

#18 Change Three Things

Therapeutic Objective
To foster a more acute visual sense of detail, memory, and spatial relations

Activity
Ask the child to look at a group of items, such as objects on a desk or dinner table. Allow him to touch the objects, turning them over in his hands and exploring their texture. Then, have the child close his eyes while you move three of the items. For example, you might move the salt shaker, pepper shaker, and sugar bowl from the right to the left side of the table, or move a stapler, paperclip holder, and pencil cup to a new location on the desk.

The child has to tell you which three items have been moved. Then, switch roles and allow the child to move the items. Begin with a small group of items; as the child becomes more adept, add more objects to the group.

More to Think About
To vary this game, ask the child to study the group of objects for a specified amount of time. Then, have him cover his eyes while you remove and hide one item. The child has to guess which item is missing.

#19 Counting Race

Therapeutic Objective

To strengthen attention and concentration skills

Activity

In this counting exercise, you and the child first choose what will be counted. Maybe you will count everything in the room that is brown, anything made out of metal, anything round, or anything soft. You can take turns deciding what you will count. Then, decide the length of time you have to count the items. Whoever has counted the most in the allotted time will be the winner.

Counting Race can be varied to make it easier or more challenging. To make it easier, work together and count the items with the child, or go on a hunt to find the specific items. To make it more challenging, write a list of the items you each found, or create a graph that compares how many of each item you found.

More to Think About

Counting is a way to make sense of the world around us. This exercise blends focusing, identifying, and counting in the format of a race, and can be played anywhere. In a car, ask the child to select something to count, such as red cars, exit signs, or trucks. On a bus or train, the child can count stop signs along the way. Walking outdoors, the child might count all the people carrying bags, wearing blue, or holding umbrellas.

Another spin-off on this activity would be to ask the child to predict how many items he thinks he will find in a specific category in one minute. Then, time the child and see if his prediction was correct.

#20 "I Went into the Woods and Heard..."

Therapeutic Objective
To strengthen the child's auditory processing skills, memory, and attention span

Activity
This activity can be played with two or more people. The first person says, "I went into the woods and heard..." and then makes a sound. It can be a commonly recognized sound, such as 'Quack! Quack!' or a made-up sound, such as 'Beloop!' Players can use their voices, clap their hands, snap their fingers, or make sounds in any other creative way.

The next person says, "I went into the woods and heard 'Quack! Quack!' (saying the first person's sound) and I heard 'Crunch.'" Each person takes a turn remembering all the previous sounds in the correct order and then adding a new sound to the list. When one person cannot remember the entire sequence or imitate it, he is out of the game.

More to Think About
An easier variation on the above activity is to take turns making a sound in a specific rhythm, which the other person must copy as best he can. Snapping, clapping, singing, humming, stamping feet, knocking on a door—any sound can be used, as long as the player uses it to create a rhythm or pattern.

#21 Conversations

Therapeutic Objective

To develop the child's conversational skills by strengthening his thought processes and encouraging him to practice proper sequencing

Activity

Each person decides on a sentence. It can be any sentence he wants, as long as the two players' sentences have nothing to do with each other. Then, the person chosen to go first begins the conversation with his selected sentence. The players go back and forth, having a conversation that can cover any topic. At the end of the game, the second person must use his original sentence to finish the conversation. The idea of this activity is that the second person must try to direct the conversation to a logical conclusion that will allow him to fit in his chosen sentence.

More to Think About

You can choose to have logical conversations that make sense or engage in silly conversations. To vary this activity, engage the child in a conversation where you are only allowed to ask questions. Take turns asking each other a question and answering with another question.

#22 Treasure Hunt

Therapeutic Objective
To encourage the internalization of structure and routine

Activity
Make a list of at least ten items in your immediate environment. Be as specific as possible, for example, a red shoe with laces, a yellow bowl, a book about bunnies, a leaf from a tree, and so on. If the child cannot read, give him a picture list. The child's task is to find and retrieve these objects. The most important rule is that he must follow the order of the list in finding each item and bringing it back to a designated spot. If, for example, the child finds the fifth item before spotting the second item, he is not permitted to retrieve it. By following the sequence on the list, the child is learning to focus on and complete one task at a time. When the child finds and retrieves all the items in sequence, you can reward him with something fun, such as playing a game of his choice.

More to Think About
This activity can help a child complete a series of responsibilities. For example, give the child a list of tasks that must be done before he boards the school bus in the morning. Begin with just a few (brush teeth, brush hair) and gradually add on (brush teeth, brush hair, wash face, get dressed, eat breakfast). As you reinforce the idea that the child must focus on one thing before moving on to the next task, you are also encouraging the internalization of structure and routine.

To make this activity more physical for a kinesthetic learner, you can make a list of tasks that must be performed in sequential order. The tasks can be practical or silly—from tying your shoelace to hopping like a rabbit to doing a cartwheel.

#23 Follow the Map

Therapeutic Objective
To develop the child's ability to follow directions

Activity
First, write a series of directions that describe how to go from one place to the next. If the child cannot read, be sure to tell him the directions clearly. You can make the directions silly, such as "Spin like a top across the room," or more commonplace, such as "Take three baby steps." For example, if you are using this activity at home, you might write: "Begin in the kitchen. Take two baby steps out of the kitchen. Turn to the left. Take two giant steps forward. Turn to the right. Hop forward three hops. Where are you?"

The child will now be in a new location. Either end the activity at that location, or leave a new set of directions that the child must follow to get to the next place. You can also leave a reward at the end.

More to Think About
Another fun way to play this is to draw a map. Put an "X" at the starting and finishing points. Draw footprints on the map. For example, you might draw two footprints in a vertical line, and then draw five more footprints turned to the left. See if the child can follow the map by taking the number of steps the map indicates. You can also vary this activity by asking the child to estimate how many steps it will take to get from one place to the next, and then try to get there in that many steps.

To do this activity, the child must listen to, or carefully read, directions and pay attention. If he misses a step, he will not be able to follow the map successfully.

#24 Listen Up!

Therapeutic Objective

To reinforce the concept of following a sequence of commands and encourage the breaking down of tasks into smaller steps

Activity

The child will decide on a task—for example, stacking blocks, putting ice into a glass of water, or tying a shoelace—and write a series of detailed instructions to accomplish that task. For younger children, you can take dictation. Once the instructions are written down, the child has to follow them exactly to accomplish the specific task. If the child cannot read, read each step to him.

More to Think About

This activity helps the child better understand the concept of instructions—and he'll be relieved to know he'll be the one to make up the instructions! It is not as easy as it may seem. For example, if the task is to put a toy in the closet but the door is shut, the child will have to verbalize each step: turn the door knob, open the door, find a space to place the toy, etc.

At home, keep a folder or notebook with all the instructions the child writes or dictates. When you need him to do one of the tasks, take out his "instruction manual" and let him follow his own lead. He is likely to be more responsive to his own directions.

CHAPTER 3:
For Identifying and Verbalizing Feelings

Children often have difficulty reading emotions, both their own and others'. A child with A.D.H.D. may act on an impulse without understanding the feeling attached to the action. For example, the child might lash out or hit when frustrated. Instead of verbalizing disappointment, the child might withdraw emotionally. Learning to respond in a direct and appropriate manner will help a child become more verbally assertive, rather than aggressive or passive.

Many children are unaware of the meaning of body language, voice intonation, and facial responses. Their personal interactions and relationships suffer greatly, because they do not pick up on social cues. Children who ignore or misinterpret social cues will either not respond or will react inappropriately. Some kids will become so engrossed in what they are talking about that they ignore the reactions of those they are speaking with. Other kids are so excited about what they are saying that they impulsively interrupt others who are talking. Children may also react to others sincerely, but in a blunt manner that lacks sensitivity and forethought.

The following activities strengthen skills that will help children in their interpersonal relationships: identifying, monitoring, and modulating their feelings, and more openly expressing concern, affection, and empathy towards others.

#25 Faces and Gestures

Therapeutic Objective

To foster social skills and increase the child's ability to express his feelings through facial expression and body language

Activity

Take turns making faces and using body language to show different feelings. One player must guess which emotion the other player is expressing. You can also both try to communicate the same emotion, and decide whose facial expression or body language best conveys the feeling.

More to Think About

The ability to interpret facial expressions and body language is important in understanding how people feel. For example, a frown communicates sadness, a smile usually signifies happiness, and arms crossed over one's chest mean anger or defiance.

If a child is having a difficult time verbalizing his feelings, you might ask him to use a facial expression or gesture to help clue you in to his mood. While playing this game, take the opportunity to ask the child to show you the facial expression that best reflects his general mood that day. Parents can use this activity to find out more about their child's feelings after a day at school, after a play date or after any positive or negative experience.

#26 Drawing Egg Heads

Therapeutic Objective
To help the child identify, integrate, and articulate a variety of feelings

Activity
Draw twenty ovals on a piece of paper. Using crayons, markers, or collage materials, take turns drawing a face in each one. Give each face a name that corresponds to the feeling it depicts. Tape up the paper and ask the child to point to the face that best illustrates his mood. Then, ask him to point to the one he thinks best illustrates his teacher's mood, a friend's mood, or a family member's mood for that day.

More to Think About
This activity is great for helping a child become more aware of the range and variety of emotional states. Children often mistake one feeling for another. For example, a child might think he is bored when he is feeling lonely. He may think he feels anger when he is disappointed. Using artwork, this activity helps define feelings by identifying, labeling and verbalizing them. It is also a fun activity, which can be done anywhere that paper and pencils are available.

#27 Feelings Stories

Therapeutic Objective

To enable the child to better identify his feelings and educate him about the wide range of feelings people experience

Activity

On separate slips of paper, write five to ten different feelings, such as: sad, mad, glad, happy, shy, frustrated, proud, excited, surprised, frightened, and confused. The list of feelings on page 74 can provide you with additional ideas. Put the slips of paper into a hat. Pick one and ask the child to pick one. Then, take turns making up a brief story about someone who feels that way. The child can write his story or dictate it to you, and then illustrate it or act it out.

More to Think About

This activity can be a great jumpstart for conversations about different feelings and situations in which people experience those feelings. It is important to help the child understand that feelings are neither good nor bad, right nor wrong.

For an easier variation, take turns miming the feelings written on the cards and guessing which feeling is being acted out. You can also tape-record the child telling his story, so he can listen to it whenever he wants.

#28 Feelings Journal

Therapeutic Objective
To strengthen the child's expressive skills and ability to identify and share his feelings

Activity
Give the child a drawing pad or staple some paper together. Write a different feeling on top of each page. When the child seems to be experiencing a particular feeling, try to identify it verbally and encourage the child to use the corresponding page in his journal. If a child is becoming increasingly frustrated during an activity, you can diffuse his frustration by encouraging him to write a poem or draw a picture of a child involved in the same activity.

More to Think About
Encourage the child to use his journal in a way that best allows him to express himself. He can write about the feeling, write about a specific time he experienced that feeling, or draw a picture depicting it.

At home, keep the journal in a place easily accessible to the child, but be sure to value his privacy!

#29 Simon Says—with Feelings

Therapeutic Objective
To expand the child's understanding of emotions

Activity
This activity is a variation on the classic game of "Simon Says." In this version, the person chosen to be Simon gives directions that relate to emotions, such as: "Simon says, show me a surprised face," "Simon says, show me a sad face," or "Show me a scared person." The other player must follow Simon's directions, but only when they are preceded by the words, "Simon says…" Take turns being Simon.

More to Think About
Although they often talk about feeling sad, happy, or mad, children need to learn that there is a broader range of emotions they may experience. They may feel frustrated, but say they are angry. They may feel lonely, but appear bored. The more feelings they can identify, the easier it will be for them to appropriately express their moods, so be sure to use varied emotions. The list on page 74 provides suggestions.

#30 Can You Hear?

Therapeutic Objective
To help the child develop more appropriate reactions by deciphering voice sounds and tones

Activity
Using a tape recorder, you can record each other making a variety of sounds that convey different emotions. Ask the child to pretend he is crying, laughing, feeling angry, humming a happy tune, enjoying a delicious piece of pie, etc. The only rule is that the child may not use words. He must identify a feeling and then create a sound that reflects the feeling—for example, Yummy! Ouch! Aargh! Psst! After taping the sounds, listen to them together and ask the child to identify the feelings portrayed.

More to Think About
Children love to hear themselves on tape, and the sounds they make are clues to their feelings. The more a child focuses on feelings, the easier it will be for him to identify his own and others' feelings. To provide more practice, save the tape and take it out another day. Try to guess what feelings you were each expressing on the tape.

This game can be played anywhere, at any time, even without access to a tape recorder. Just take turns making sounds that go along with feelings; then, guess the feelings.

#31 Feelings Photos

Therapeutic Objective

To teach children to use body language to express feelings and to practice their identification of feelings

Activity

Take pictures of the child in a variety of poses that depict different feelings. For example, he might look frightened, excited, nervous, or brave. See how many poses the child can think up and act out for each feeling. When the pictures are developed, put them in a photo album or tape them on paper, giving each one a title. These pictures can be used to help the child identify his own or others' feelings.

An instant camera is particularly good for this activity, giving the child the immediate gratification of seeing the picture in minutes. If you don't have access to a camera, take turns posing for a pretend photo shoot. Each pose should depict a different feeling, which the other person must guess.

More to Think About

This is an experiential activity that helps a child use an external pose to access internal feelings. The more aware a child becomes of the connection between his internal and external environment, the easier it will be for him to identify his own feelings and express them assertively.

If you are doing this activity at home, browse through old family photos and try to assess what family members were feeling at the time the picture was taken. What in the picture clued the child in to the feelings portrayed?

#32 What Do I Feel?

Therapeutic Objective

To enable children to reflect on feelings and understand the reaction of others to different stimuli

Activity

Take turns giving hints about what you feel. The other person has to guess the chosen feeling.

> For example: I feel this way when I ride my bicycle.
> I feel this way when you give me a hug.
> I feel this way when I do well at school.

> What do I feel? (The answer might be happy or confident.)

You are allowed up to three hints; give one at a time until the other person figures out the feeling.

More to Think About

This activity helps a child to understand his own feelings, and to experience the world from another person's perspective. It can help children strengthen their interpersonal skills and learn to read another person's clues to their own internal process.

#33 I Spy—with Feelings

Therapeutic Objective

To make the child more aware of his emotional reactions by linking them to objects in his environment

Activity

This game is similar to activity #32. However, this time you are using the immediate environment to help the child identify his feelings. For example, if you "spy" a vase of flowers, you can say, "I spy something in this room that makes me very happy when I smell it." The other person has three chances to guess; after three guesses, another player has a turn.

More to Think About

This activity is both internal and external. It may be especially beneficial for a child who needs help developing his visual skills and linking what he sees to how he feels.

At home, this activity can help reorient a child to his bedroom and foster a positive bedtime. If the child has difficulty falling asleep, you can suggest that he play this game by himself while lying in bed, looking around the room and connecting objects to how they make him feel.

#34 No Words Allowed

Therapeutic Objective
To improve the child's skill at assessing nonverbal interaction

Activity
Watch the child's favorite television show with him, but mute the sound. Ask the child to try to guess the actors' feelings by looking at their facial expressions and body gestures. What are the actors' relationships with one another? Why does he think this? What does he think their tone of voice is? How would he describe this scene? Guess what kind of background music might be playing, and then turn up the sound to see if you are correct.

More to Think About
This is a rich exercise, filled with a variety of learning experiences and very beneficial in heightening a child's awareness of others' feelings. By becoming more attuned to others, the child will be better able to read other people's signals. Practice in reading another person's gestures and visual cues will also help a child become more empathetic and compassionate.

#35 Favorite Memories

Therapeutic Objective

To enable the child to identify and express feelings regarding his unique life events

Activity

Ask the child to remember a favorite trip or activity, such as building a sand castle, playing basketball, or going on a ride at the amusement park. Who was with the child? What did he do there? Why was it so positive? Find a photo of the place, or have the child draw a picture.

Brainstorm and list positive memories of the trip or activity. What made it so much fun? Is it realistic and reasonable to do this again? If it is an activity you can plan to repeat, put it on a calendar and remind the child of the upcoming date or time. If it is not realistic to reexperience, enjoy sharing the memory together.

More to Think About

Keep a scrapbook of the child's best memories—a ticket stub from a favorite movie, a beautiful autumn leaf, a photo of the child with a special friend or a relative. When the child needs to calm down, take out his memory book and look through it together. Bring the book with you to places that you know will trigger difficulty for the child, such as waiting for a doctor's appointment, sitting still at a restaurant, or going on a long car ride.

CHAPTER 4:
For Building Self-Esteem and Confidence

Children with A.D.D or A.D.H.D. are at an increased risk for low self-esteem. They are constantly being bombarded with negative messages: You're not sitting still...You're not listening...Stop fidgeting...Stop touching...Don't interrupt...I've told you a thousand times...Can't you be more like your sister, and so on.

Children want to stop misbehaving. They want to do better and behave more appropriately, but they may not understand the link between their own excessive or inappropriate behavior and the rejection or negative signals others direct towards them. Over time, their feelings of self-worth plummet.

Self-esteem comes from an internalized, positive self-image, which stems from consistent nurturing, encouragement, boundaries, and positive reinforcement—and from a realistic set of adult expectations. Knowing the child's innate nature, capabilities, and developmental level will help adults to construct appropriate expectations. Once adults adjust their own expectations, children are often given more room to thrive, while feeling more accepted.

Everybody has positive qualities, as well as difficult traits. Often children tend to focus on the negative aspects of their personalities or behavior and forget about the good, but it is never too late to develop a strong positive attitude about oneself. By teaching a child to behave in prosocial ways and get positive feedback from others, the activities in this chapter help a child internalize positive self-esteem.

#36 Compliments and Praise

Therapeutic Objective

To encourage the child to focus on his positive qualities, rather than his more negative or troublesome behaviors

Activity

Ask the child to name three things he thinks he does well. Have him write or draw them on paper. At home, plan time in the upcoming week to do more of these things. Take a picture of the child engaging in an activity he feels good about and send it to a grandparent or friend. Now, tell the child three things you think he does well, and three reasons why you like him. Be sure to praise the child for all the positive behaviors you notice.

More to Think About

If you are using this activity at home, you may want to plan for a daily meeting with the child where you tell him all the positive behaviors you noticed that day. Be as specific as possible. For example: I was proud of you when you shared your toys with your brother, and when you cleaned up your room. It only takes a few minutes to praise a child, but the effects are long-lasting.

You can also plan for a specific time during the week when the child will show you something he thinks he does well. It can be anything from tying his shoelaces to skateboarding, singing a song, dancing, drawing, or counting. Be sure that the child chooses on his own what he will share with you, and of course, applaud his efforts with praise.

#37 What's Inside Me?

Therapeutic Objective

To enable the adult to identify and assess the child's experience of himself

Activity

Have the child lie down on a large piece of paper or newsprint. Using a crayon or marker, trace his entire outline—including head, torso, legs, and arms—for the child to fill in. He may feel more comfortable filling in the outline realistically, drawing eyes, a nose, and a mouth on the face, buttons on the shirt, and shoes on the feet. You can also encourage the child to draw the way he feels about himself in a more expressive way, perhaps by drawing butterflies in his stomach or gluing magazine pictures onto the outline. The child can also write words inside the outline.

More to Think About

The important part of this activity is to emphasize that the picture is one of the child, created uniquely by him. Display the child's picture, and encourage him to think of it as a "work in progress." When he comes home from school, the child may want to add to the picture or take something off. A constantly transforming picture reflects the fact that people are always changing.

#38 Seeing Success

Therapeutic Objective
To focus the child's attention on past accomplishments and future goals

Activity
Ask the child to think of a goal he would like to achieve. His goal might range from learning to skip rope to making more friends or receiving a better grade on his next quiz. Whatever the child expresses as the goal should be taken seriously.

Picturing success is the first step in reaching one's goal, so have the child close his eyes and see "success" in his mind. Ask him to concentrate on whatever it is he wants to achieve, seeing it as a detailed and clear mental movie. Suggest that he imagine, from beginning to end, how he could reach his goal. Together, make a list of the steps he must take to reach his goal. Or, you can draw a picture of a staircase, write the goal on the top step, and label each step from the bottom up with an action leading to the goal.

More to Think About
Showing a child how many things he has already accomplished successfully will help him see and feel his own competency. Success doesn't just happen; children learn to make it happen. Make a list of successes the child has already achieved—learning to tie his shoes, ride a bike, read, and write—and celebrate those successes together. Then, look at each success and break it down into smaller, specific steps. This exercise can help the child recognize the individual steps along the way to reaching his goals.

#39 Mirror Me

Therapeutic Objective

To foster the child's attention span and increase his awareness of the reciprocal nature of relationships

Activity

Sit across from the child, and take turns being the leader. The leader makes a facial expression, hand gesture, or subtle body movement. The other player tries to become a mirror image, making the same movement as the leader at the same time. Be sure to begin with simple actions—touching your nose or blinking your eyes—that the child can mirror easily. You can progress to more complex actions, such as brushing teeth, combing hair, or catching and throwing a ball.

You can also use verbal activities, in which the leader makes a sound, utters a short phrase or says a full sentence. The mirror image then tries to copy the sound with the exact intonation.

More to Think About

If you are playing with more than one child, you can all sit in a circle. The activity is played the same way as with two people, except that you pass the movement around the circle. The first person initiates a movement, which the second person tries to mirror. The second person then turns to the third person and reflects the same movement. The third person turns to the fourth person, or back to the first person who creates a new movement to be mirrored.

When the child initiates the movements, the activity helps increase self-esteem, identifying him as a being who creates an impact on those around him. It also instills a sense of leadership, which helps to build a positive self-image.

#40 Greeting Cards

Therapeutic Objective
To encourage gratitude, compassion, and self-esteem

Activity
Have the child create greeting cards to send to friends and family members. These cards can be long or short, serious or humorous. They can rhyme or not. It is up to the child to decide how to word his card and how to decorate it.

Ask the child to think of a person towards whom he has positive feelings. What does he especially like about this person? What does he feel like when he is with this person? How does this person help him feel good? What would he like to say to the person? He can write his feelings about the person in the card or just discuss his feelings with you. If the child is uncertain about what kind of card to write, you can suggest a "thank-you" card. Ask the child to think of something the other person has given him, shared with him, or taught him. Emphasize that this card is not necessarily a thank-you for material things, but for a special experience, a good time, or someone's unique way of caring about him.

More to Think About
You might want to take turns talking about one or two special things you do to make other people feel good, comfortable, or loved. If the child is having a difficult time verbalizing his own positive qualities, help him by naming a few positive characteristics that make him a person worth knowing. Perhaps you can focus on his sense of humor, zest for adventure, or interesting outlook on life. Maybe you, as the adult, would like to write a thank-you note to the child. Be sure to be honest and direct.

Then, ask the child to write a thank-you note to himself for something he has done to make himself feel good, something he has accomplished, or something he likes about himself.

#41 Feelings Walk

Therapeutic Objective

To help the child better identify and express his feelings and become more aware of the emotions of others

Activity

Explain to the child that this exercise is like acting. First, the child will be himself. He will walk around the room and express the way he truly feels at that moment. Perhaps he feels sad, glad, mad, or silly. Perhaps he doesn't know what he feels, which is okay. After about one minute, tell the child to "freeze." When he unfreezes, he will choose a new feeling to "try on" and experience as he walks around the room. After a few different feelings, ask the child to return to being himself. Suggest the child give himself a big hug to appreciate his uniqueness.

More to Think About

This experiential exercise can be a helpful jumpstart for many conversations. Some questions to explore are: What did it feel like to walk around the room feeling different from yourself? How did your body language and facial expressions change with each new feeling? Was one feeling more pleasant than another? How did it feel to then be yourself again?

#42 Color Talk

Therapeutic Objective
To use color as a nonthreatening vehicle for self-exploration and self-expression

Activity
Prepare a set of index cards with a single color blot on each one. Ask the child to pick a card and discuss what the color means to him. What does it remind him of? How many things of that color can he name? Can he move like the color? Sing like the color? What mood does the color make him feel? What is the child's favorite color? Why? Think of as many words as possible to describe colors, such as brilliant, murky, dull, shiny, harsh, or pale. Make up your own words for different colors. End the activity by asking the child to write a sensory poem about a chosen color. You can use the following format, filling in the blanks with words describing a specific color.

(Title)

I see _____

I hear _____

I smell _____

I taste _____

The color _____ makes me feel _____.

More to Think About
Think about phrases that use color to describe feelings, such as red with anger or green with envy. How many songs or rhymes can the child think of that use color? Some examples are: "Baa, Baa, Black Sheep," "Mary had a little lamb whose fleece was white as snow," and "Yellow

Submarine." Together, make up your own songs with colorful lyrics.

Listen to different types of music together. What colors do the lyrics and melodies remind you of? The child can make a "color response," by drawing a picture of his feelings about a particular piece of music, using only one color.

#43 Who Am I?

Therapeutic Objective

To help the child build positive feelings about himself and recognize his own uniqueness

Activity

Ask the child to cut out pictures or words from magazines or newspapers that best describe who he is. Have him make a collage with the material. He can paste the cutouts on a cardboard box, a notebook cover, or a piece of paper. This project is the child's, and there is no right or wrong way for him to describe himself. If you make suggestions, make them positive and loving.

Some questions to help the child think about himself are: What characteristics make you special? What kinds of things do you like to do? What are your favorite foods? Where do you live? Where do your grandparents come from? What's your favorite color? Favorite story? Favorite song? What kinds of friends do you choose?

More to Think About

Have the child paste or glue images cut from magazines onto a photograph of himself to create a silly or interesting photo. For example, he might glue on a hat, sunglasses, a different body, or animal ears onto his photograph.

#44 My Emotional Bank Account

Therapeutic Objective
To build self-esteem and create a more nurturing family environment

Activity
At home, keep a box in a shared part of the home, such as the kitchen. This box is the child's "emotional bank account." Ask him to write positive words describing himself and put the slips of paper into the box. Remind him to write down his own feelings of success. He can write notes stating that he shared his toys, cleaned up his room, or did his homework without a complaint, or he can write words such as "giving," "helpful," etc. If the child is too young to write, he can draw a picture or tell you the words. You can add to the account also. Whenever the child acts in a positive, appropriate, or constructive manner, write it down and deposit it. Every few days, open the box and read the slips of paper together.

More to Think About
Have the child ask as many people as he can to list his best qualities. Write them down and post the paper in a place that he will often see it. Read it every day. You can also put this list into his emotional bank account.

#45 Personal Charity Drive

Therapeutic Objective
To teach compassion, empathy, and appreciation through acts of giving

Activity
At home, collect old toys that the child no longer plays with and clothes that he has outgrown. Make a pile of the items he is willing to give to a local organization that accepts such donations. The power of giving is felt most significantly if the child is able to experience handing the items to the organization or people, so the more hands-on, the better. Praise the child for his generosity and willingness to help others.

Another activity is to have the child make a list of helpful things he can do around the house. Rather than jobs or responsibilities, encourage the child to list deeds that come from a spirit of generosity to help or create happiness in someone else. They can be simple acts, like helping another family member with a project, clearing off the dinner table, or leaving a note saying "I love you" on someone's pillow.

More to Think About
Self-esteem flourishes when a child behaves appropriately and is encouraged and complimented for achievements. Self-esteem also grows when children learn to be charitable. This activity focuses on what a child can do for others, rather than on what he is able to gain. You might create a family tradition of spending some time helping others, such as a particular day each month or year when you help out at a local soup kitchen, homeless shelter, hospital, or place of worship.

Another idea is to create a family charity box for loose change. Suggest that the child give a portion of his allowance money to the charity box. At the end of every month, decide as a family to which charity you will donate the money.

#46 Clean-Up Race

Therapeutic Objective
To enable the child to earn adult approval by being neat and organized

Activity
This activity is for younger children who forget to clean up after themselves. When it is time for the child to put his toys away, challenge him to a clean-up race. Tell the child you are going to time him to see how quickly he can clean up his toys. You can even record the time, so that he can try to do better the next day.

Clean-Up Race is an easy activity to do even when the child has a friend over to play. They can race to see who can finish putting the toys away first. Competition can be a great incentive!

More to Think About
This activity helps the child learn to meet adult expectations by tidying up after himself at home and by being a good guest. In a fun way, you are reinforcing the importance of being a well-mannered guest.

A good way to minimize mess and create structure is by labeling all storage shelves, cabinets, or drawers with words or pictures, so that the child knows exactly where to place items.

47 Look at Me Look at You

Therapeutic Objective

To help the child pick up significant social cues through eye contact

Activity

Sit facing the child and look into one another's eyes. Whoever averts their eyes first loses the round. For variation, you can decide on other rules together. Blinking may or may not be allowed. Giggling may or may not be allowed. Whoever blinks, or giggles, first loses the round.

More to Think About

Bend down so that your eyes are at the same level as the child's. You may notice that his eyes dart around, not focusing on your eyes. If the child doesn't focus on faces or eyes, he's probably missing the smiles and frowns of his peers, family members, and teachers. As a result, he may not behave appropriately in a given situation. Eye contact is an essential part of social interactions, which are so important to self-esteem. When a child he is having a conversation, meeting new people, or listening to others speak, he should be expected to sustain eye contact.

#48 Obstacle Course

Therapeutic Objective
To enhance self-esteem by developing the child's sense of competency and mastery

Activity
The goal of this activity is for the child to complete an obstacle course from beginning to end. You can work with the child to create the course, which may be simple or challenging. You might put a few pillows in a row, and have the child start the course by hopping or jumping from pillow to pillow, and then climbing through a play tunnel or under a table. Next, the child might have to jump rope three times before walking backwards towards you.

Be creative; there is no right or wrong way to make an obstacle course.

More to Think About
This activity is great to play outside, even in a playground. There are an infinite number of obstacles you can create for, or with, the child. The obstacle course can be played together, or you can race. If there are more than two people playing, you can divide the children into teams.

Obstacle Course has the potential of invigorating and energizing both you and the child. As long as the child stays on course, he is learning to use his energy purposefully and staying focused.

CHAPTER 5:
For Channeling and Releasing Excess Energy Appropriately

This chapter is about release of energy. These activities do not necessarily emphasize calming down an overly aroused child; instead they are alternative activities that are appropriate outlets for channeling excess energy. Unlike Chapter 1, which emphasized internal and external body awareness and control, this chapter emphasizes more direct diversions for restlessness and hyperactivity. A child may wander from toy to toy, engaging only momentarily in whatever has caught his attention. Overstimulated by his own hyperactive state, he may escalate to an even more frenetic level. This chapter will enable you to help the child prevent this escalation. Consistent use of the following activities serves two purposes: to deflect from the child's negative behavior and to redirect the child by offering a more appropriate expression of his heightened activity level.

There are many outlets for releasing excess energy. Channeled appropriately, high energy is a wonderful asset. It is highly recommended that a child who exhibits hyperactive tendencies be involved in sports. Whatever sport the child is attracted to can serve the purpose, whether it is skating, soccer, basketball, hockey, or swimming. If it is an appropriate physical outlet, use it. At home, other options include purchasing equipment such as a small trampoline, a punching bag and gloves, or even just an old tire tied to a tree for the child to hang and swing on. These things will do wonders for an impulsive or hyperactive child.

49 Water Painting

Therapeutic Objective
To develop the child's tactile sense

Activity
Give the child a paintbrush, or a few brushes of different sizes, and a pail of water. If you are outside, let him paint the house by brushing water onto the siding, or paint the fence or the street. You can also use this activity at bath time by adding bubbles to the child's bath water. Let the child paint the tiles with the bubbles.

More to Think About
Water play is a wonderful way for a child to release his energy and feel less fidgety and restless. Washing dishes with soapy water in the kitchen sink will engage a child whose energies are chaotic, but be sure not to give the child any dishes that might break. You can also bring a bottle of water to a sandbox. Mixing sand and water serves to create new textures that will engage the child. Washing the car with a pail of water, sponges, and a hose engages the child's entire body and helps him release energy purposefully.

#50 Paper Shred and Toss

Therapeutic Objective
To enable the child to work out anger and aggression appropriately

Activity
Offer the child a few large garbage bags and a variety of paper, ranging from newspaper to cardboard, tracing paper, and construction paper. Ask the child to rip the paper into as many shreds as possible. After the paper is shredded, have the child stuff the garbage bags and tie a knot closing the bag. Now, toss the bags back and forth to one another. Ask the child to notice which bag is heavier. Can he catch it? Does it bounce?

You can race to see who fills the bags first, or time the child to see how quickly he can shred the paper and stuff the bags.

More to Think About
Keep a pile of newspapers always available. When you see that the child is agitated or overly aroused, redirect him to the newspaper and plastic bag pile. Eventually, he will learn to redirect himself independently.

This activity also works well for an angry child, who can release some of his anger by ripping the paper and throwing it into bags. After the bags are filled, he can punch them.

#51 Blowing Bubbles

Therapeutic Objective

To encourage relaxation and calmness by allowing the child to dispel excess energy

Activity

Ask the child to blow bubbles, and explain that before he is permitted to pop the bubble, he has to follow some directions. Give him varied directions before each pop of the bubble. For example: Jump in place three times, and then pop one bubble. Turn in a circle, and then pop two bubbles. You can make the directions as easy or challenging as the child can handle. Ask him to imagine that each bubble he blows is taking a little bit of his excess energy as it floats away. With each bubble popped, the child's energy level becomes more organized and manageable.

More to Think About

Blowing bubbles helps release energy. If you do not have bubbles and a wand, you can use items around the house, such as soapy water and a straw. The child can try to pop the bubble with his elbows, feet, chin, or the top of his head. He can try to blow the bubbles through things, over things and under things, and see which bubbles float farthest. What happens when he blows softly? When he blows hard? He might find that using softer breath makes the bubble bigger and better. Explain how being in control means being gentle...and being gentle reaps big rewards.

For a more educational twist, you can ask a younger child to try writing his name before popping the bubble. An older child may have to do a simple math equation.

#52 Beat the Clock

Therapeutic Objective
To enhance the child's sense of mastery and competence

Activity
Run around a tree. Crawl from one side of the room to the other. Hop to the kitchen. Score three baskets in the basketball hoop. How fast can you tie a shoelace? How quickly can you run to the corner and back? How long can you stand on your head?

With the child, take turns creating a variety of races. They can be silly or serious. They can be a physical or mental challenge. Then, either set a timer for a certain amount of time in which you expect the child to finish the task, or time him to see how long it takes. Can he accomplish the task in five seconds? One minute? Can he beat the clock? Is he faster the second time he tries, or the third?

More to Think About
Instead of trying to subdue excess energy, this activity invites energy, enthusiasm, and motivation. Each race is purposeful, with a task to be completed. Rather than focusing on the child's negative behavior, try to redirect him to this activity, which will pull him away from distracted and purposeless activity to a more focused but active challenge. You might even try using this activity when you want the child to clean up his room or his toys. Tell him that he has to try to beat the clock by cleaning up in a certain amount of time. Making the chore a fast and fun-filled race might spark his initiative.

#53 Superhero

Therapeutic Objective
To help the child recognize his potential and identify his assets

Activity
Ask the child to pretend to be a superhero. He can make up his own superhero or be one that he's read about or seen on television. Why does he like this superhero? What does this hero do? How do his actions help others? Make a list of all the good qualities of the superhero, and ask if the child shares some of these qualities. If the child has difficulty making a long list, ask him to name just two things about the superhero. Have him draw a picture of the superhero, and put on a cape and pretend to be the superhero.

Ask the child what he would most like his superhero to help him with. What would he want the superhero to do for others?

More to Think About
If the child's behavior becomes inappropriate, ask him to reflect on how his superhero would act. What can the child do to try to be more like his superhero in the situation? Sometimes, just reminding the child about the superhero he created will propel him into more positive behavior.

#54 Balancing Acts

Therapeutic Objective
To stimulate motor coordination, focus, concentration, and self-control

Activity
Set out a selection of objects, such as a book, a spoon, a plastic cup, and a small toy, and ask the child to see how many different objects he can balance. First, ask him to balance an object on his head. Can he walk forward while balancing the objects? What about walking backward or sideways? Ask him to try balancing an object on each of his palms, with his arms extended to the sides. Can he balance an object on the back of his hand? On the top of his feet? Ask him to bend over and try to balance the object on his back... standing on one foot...with his eyes closed. Is it much more difficult to balance things now? Have him try to balance one or two objects on his back, while walking across the room on all fours like a cat. Ask him to walk in a straight line, and then in a zig-zag. Can he balance a feather on the tip of his finger or on his chin?

More to Think About
This activity takes some concentration and coordination. It is especially helpful in developing the child's ability to maintain his equilibrium in a variety of situations. By using different muscle groups, the activity strengthens his gross motor skills.

#55 Trust Walk

Therapeutic Objective
To build trust and foster greater attention to body awareness

Activity
With his eyes closed, lead the child around his environment. Speak softly and gently guide the child around the house or room, on or over soft objects, such as pillows, or through a play tunnel. Do everything you can to make the child feel secure; safety and trust are foremost! Avoid steps or any place where the child could be hurt.

Now, switch roles and let the child guide you. Let him know that you feel more secure when he is careful and thinks about how he is guiding you. Explain that the more caution he uses, the more comfortable you feel.

More to Think About
Discuss what would have happened if you had not told the child to step up or down or around various objects. What would the physical consequences have been? What other consequences are there? What does this activity have to do with trust?

#56 Be Silent

Therapeutic Objective
To develop attentional skills and increase frustration tolerance

Activity
The goal of this activity is to give the child a focus when his activity level is otherwise unfocused. There are two rules: you each must be completely silent, and you cannot communicate through written messages. When someone breaks the silence, the game is over.

After the silence is broken, discuss what it felt like to be silent. Was it challenging? Frustrating? Relaxing? Could the child fulfill his needs? Could you understand him?

More to Think About
You can try this game with lip reading. Take turns talking without making any sounds and see if you can understand one another. To play this game, the child must use a variety of important skills, including eye contact, thought processing, body language, and facial expressions.

List of Feelings

Affectionate	Irritable
Aggravated	Jealous
Angry	Joyful
Ashamed	Kind
Attentive	Lazy
Brave	Lonely
Cautious	Loving
Challenged	Mad
Cheerful	Mean
Confident	Nervous
Confused	Peaceful
Curious	Popular
Distracted	Proud
Dreamy	Quiet
Eager	Relaxed
Embarrassed	Sad
Envious	Satisfied
Excited	Scared
Exhausted	Selfish
Fearful	Serious
Friendly	Shocked
Frightened	Silly
Frustrated	Smart
Funny	Sorry
Generous	Stressed
Gentle	Successful
Greedy	Surprised
Grieving	Terrified
Guilty	Thoughtful
Happy	Tough
Hurried	Unsure
Hurt	Vain
Interested	Worried

Helpful Hints for Parents

1. Use structure and schedules whenever possible.

2. Use charts and rewards to focus on accomplished tasks.

3. State your request, and then disengage from all negotiations.

4. Keep your voice steady and centered.

5. Try to achieve eye contact when talking to your child.

6. Touch your child lightly to help him attend to what you are saying.

7. Keep your directives as simple and clear as possible. If necessary, write them down.

8. Follow through with what you say, including consequences.

9. Encourage physical activity, such as sports, as often as possible.

10. Provide quiet times and places in your home.

11. Love your child for who he is, not who you would like him to be.

12. Praise your child for his individuality and his attempts, as well as his accomplishments.

13. Don't compare children.

14. Explain to your child what has helped you when you feel distracted or impulsive.

15. Be a role model.

16. Say you are sorry when you are sorry. Your apology will teach your child that it's okay to make a mistake. We all do sometimes.

17. Talk to other parents with high-spirited children or join a support group or an organization such as CHADD.

18. Keep a sense of humor.

19. Schedule time away from your children.

20. Love yourself, and give yourself permission to take care of yourself.